all you expect of the road

all you expect of the road

poems by

sue nevill

Porcepic Books
an imprint of

Beach Holme Publishing
Vancouver

This book is published by Beach Holme Publishing, #226—2040 West 12th Ave., Vancouver, BC, V6J 2G2. This is a Porcepic Book.

We acknowledge the financial support of the Canada Council for the Arts, the Government of Canada through the Book Publishing Industry Development Program (BPIDP) and the assistance of the Province of British Columbia through the British Columbia Arts Council for our publishing activities and program.

The Canada Council for the Arts | Le Conseil des Arts du Canada

Editor: Joy Gugeler
Production and Design: Jen Hamilton
Cover Art: *Winter Road I* by Georgia O'Keeffe, 1963. 22$^{1/16}$″ x 18$^{1/8}$″, oil on canvas. Collection of the National Gallery of Art, Washington, D.C. Gift of the Georgia O'Keeffe Foundation. Used with permission.
Author Photo: Casey Wolf

Canadian Cataloguing in Publication Data

Nevill, Sue, 1944-
  All you expect of the road

  Poems.
  ISBN 0-88878-407-4

  I. Title.
PS8577.E764A84 2000   C811'.54   C00-910084-9
PR9199.3.N393A84 2000

To my father, whose journey was a hard one;
and to my mother, who showed us both the way.

contents

rain to dance in at midnight

primary colours

And the next thing you know
you're waltzing down Pender Street at midnight
in your green A-line dress with the mandarin collar
bare arms open to November rain

In and out of the running gutters you and he
in your best Gene Kelly style Shoes
melt to your feet your hair comes down
in torrents and you are so
young

Through a red door and up some stairs
women in trousers and short hair
women who work in upholstery plants and wear
big watches make wide space for you at a stabbed mirror
Under a blue light your boyfriend
is dancing with another man
Just to shock you he says to introduce you
to rainbows because green
is actually a boring colour
Though you aren't quite sure what
to be shocked about you feel a lie stroke your skin
and consider it carefully

Behind some orange doors long tablecloths and
bottles in brown paper bags against your ankles
The plates in front of you hold nothing you recognize
You are glad
because this is the city These frail chopsticks
frame the world the books have promised you
Strangers join your table Genet Baudelaire
You are shy but very pleased to meet them

Now it's clear to you that life
is long possibly silver that sharp edges
are exciting that you can lie naked
on the cold bones of the earth and laugh

Your friends push their chairs back to show you
dawn through black glasses You lay your heart
on the smallest empty plate and swear
you will always look for rain to dance in
at midnight

pacific composition

Outside the liquor store
the blind man is beating his dog
for the lapse which has left him
briefly dependent on strangers

The dog turns and turns in the snow
considers the icy intersection
is willing to feel guilty cannot understand
exactly what came over him

From this moment the blind man
will doubt the dog The dog will know
he cannot trust the man
or the snow

The blind man is beating his dog in the snow
awkwardly and lovingly
like a parent who does not read the papers
painfully and rhythmically
like a person who feels he is doing his duty

Trucks
pass stealthily on ice An old lady
strokes the lamp-post and hopes
for the other side of the road

On a sliding street of black bananas
and white light on crazy-paving
outside the liquor store a blind man
is clearly beating his dog

slowdancing

She's slowdancing in the sand
of the city grinding her round
mind against hard brick
She's a beat no drummer can
   wait for
               languid with exhaust
and hesitating needles
but slow
is never slow enough
                   the bells
of blood around her ankles
the only thing fresh about her
   Grass is sharp at the edge
   of sidewalks where she swings
   inches as good as miles
   when you fall like glass

Match this she says to the drummer
damping the bump of her heart
till the line is flat *Match this*
a siren chokes around the corner
This
is a dance we can all do

backrooms–1963

The woman with lye soap and illegal eyes
the woman with knitting-needle lips and
hair like coathangers answers her phone
expecting jail digs in your gut for bail money
Somebody's got to do it

Her voice holds all the minor greedy keys
She is a friend of an enemy of yours
Most of her customers are married
come back often
occasionally die

Her cigarettes are cork-tipped
The ash hangs on for hours
The hospital is full of frowning men
with clean hands and principles
They call you *murderer*
save you anyway They think
their god should turn
your heart to salt

Escaped you dream another girl
skin full of flowers blood ignorance and heat
You dream of lye soap meet
in other backrooms
You march
You march

making time

Your face is naked to this music
so cautionless that my gaze
is invasion

Your body twists and writhes
You wind the keyboard around
your wrists stroke it with your hair
Fingers hit home
on faith and hours of understanding

The rhythm you thrust to
is the one in your veins
neural and atomic
The music in this wood and bone
is the noise of your lungs shouting
  breathe for god's
  sake breathe

Sweat
drops off each note
speaks of
the sea within you

The first sea

steaming

to the man who ate all the peanuts during
p. j. perry's first set

You must have been the only child
of older parents
   chubby and thick-lensed heavily indulged
Kids probably tripped you in the playground
threw your books
into the girls' loo
You grew up grasping for solace
in unlikely places
and never smiled in your life

Between us now this bowl at table-centre
common forage small circle of community
in a splintered world

You corner it like a moody dog
reduce the social covenant to crumbs
you can't digest

Leaning toward the stage
you block my view
Your mouth widens

All the beautiful music

You want to swallow that too
     straight no chaser

superstar
(to Ted Neely)

What does it feel like to play Jesus
night after night   bluesing
the multitudes scatting at disciples
elevated in the light and dry ice
of standing ovations

20 years since the movie ended
2000 since the original production
closed to a small house
and you've come again
history portraying history
era piled on era

20 years
is a long time to dream of crosses

Did you find
you couldn't scrub the makeup from your pores
or walk a vacant street without
the ghosts of robes against your ankles
Maybe beer turned to wine one afternoon
when you least expected it and there were nights
you screamed yourself awake to feel
your arms stretched wide   a sharp pain in your side

dressed to die

The soles of your shoes
are clean
white
I believe you have flown
directly here to die
touching nothing in passing
Now you have gone as far
on this bridge
as it is possible to go

Your legs so naturally aligned
in white trousers your white
arms with palms upturned
An eccentric
sunbathing in the right-hand lane

And we
are smooth and t.v. rehearsed
We steer the traffic around you
make statements to the police
try not to look at your head because

the rest of you is so
white
We too are white
but under tight control
We're on our way to mountains
green blue and also
bigger than we are

dancer

in mid-flight

the pain

stops

one floor below

a young man pours his guts
into his cordless phone an open window
and neighbourhood sleep

Love you he cries
and lights snap on in every building

Love his voice rising
over ambient curses *please!*

Cats young men
in love and open windows The trick
is to remember faintly
enough to sympathize
not enough to wake

candlepower

4 a.m. lights
in the windows of the man suffering love
like a cramp in a phantom hand an ex-wife whose journal
is too full for words an insomniac heart
as empty as a television screen a woman whose remote control
has broken a poet who cannot sleep because the moon
is watching and a lawyer who finds days too damn short

There's a romantic trying to feel wistful a power junkie
denying the flesh a misanthrope whose anger starts work early
an optimist waiting for owls

and a blue man who cannot stop coughing a flushed woman
who has run out of dry sheets a green boy who made
his first hard dollar at midnight a jaundiced patient anticipating
scalpels and a black woman who has swallowed insults
till she has no room for tranquilizers

Sullen flames disappointed candles
shrinking into the day

suite dreams

1.

You dream you are falling down a long chalk cliff
Your feet are frozen in a chaplinesque *V*
Between them you see milky water standing reeds
and 15-second film clips of nauseating ends
scrolling so quickly you cannot choose
which death to fear first

You turn in mid-air face the cliff and concentrate
Chalk molecules take heat and grow to grains of rice
to pearls to creamy paper parachutes and you
still falling grab one
Slower   slower   till you are barely
falling at all

The films slow too
to single frames of murky depths and unsupported heights
and a cartoon woman frowning falling down
a long chalk cliff into milky water

It grabs her by the ankles

A very shallow pool

You are upright
whole after all
and feeling foolish

You reach for the VCR switch and glance around
No one has noticed

2.

You dream you are falling into a tenor saxophone
You left your frontrow seat to peer inside it see
where music really comes from

Now the sax player has breathed in and you
small as a sixteenth note are swimming in brass and blackness
The air is humid The metal walls around you hum and groan
You're afraid you'll be blown across the smoky room
into the glass of some undistinguished lite beer drinker

You climb farther up Your fingers sprout
minuscule suckers Note by note you mount
Portholes open and close above you You poke your head
through the first possible aperture and the pad slams
down

You wake suddenly
The picture of your lover framed above your bed
has fallen on you shattering

You will never get the glass out of your pillow

3.

You dream you are falling in love

Flowers are everywhere Gulls have turned to nightingales
You are eating whipped cream in delightful restaurants
You gain 100 pounds

Your lover ties a thin gold chain around your ankle
anchors you beside his house

You rise into the air with gentle dignity You are
perfectly round perfectly aloof
You are the moon

perimeters

Your province is open skies and I am leaving you
in a city floating on smoke from
other people's conflagrations I hear
there are trees in your city
How can I tell
caught in the ring-roads
that defend your heart

All I know:
in the centre of that city your breath is blistering
a flat brown river
your running shoe tracks circling
up and down its scarps
(circling always the best defence)

But tell me this much:
    when I cross this mapline will your tracks stop
    a heartbeat a gap opening
    to one straight laser of joined thought before
    your borders slam shut again
    like winter

20/20

Your city sidles out of the dense horizon paws at your arm
like a noclass lover who has managed to learn clothes but
nothing of perfume trolls the freeway exits like a sadassed
lover who knows you are leaving him before you know
anything at all

And you move into the shiny men/women who are your city
with their humid smiles and careful hair the ones who know
what they could have been
given an eyejob and a little more truth

    Weight
    of the great-to-see-you air Regret
    inherent in greenery you used to sing to

You've let years love you up in fog and soft salt blankets
when in the opposite direction roads clean as razors
could have taken you so fast so deep

You toy with the brake but it's a comfortable highway
no U-turns every exit stalled in sand
A rainbow shakes its bars at you
and the sun is setting

west
and Hollywood as usual

azimuths

1.

You are drawn
to things that can carry you away
small boats music
anything resembling
a train

In art you prefer
the faintly pencilled
horizon Your own drawings
have no frames

2.

Words do not travel well
They lose their edge
Words are no longer
a weight you carry gladly

Look
at the power of one charcoal line
extending margins

another way to saskatchewan

another way to saskatchewan

Going to Saskatchewan I write

and my friend who has seen
the odd American western
                    falls away
from constant well-hedged fields
green at all times and rimmed with may
and blackthorn except where a drystone wall
has stood for five or six centuries close to
a village anchored in oak
                    falls into S-shaped rivers
each broader than a field
rivers that hiss through banks of dust
to catch and swallow herds of narrow cattle
and excrete their bones while overhead
a sun that cannot conceive of trees
glares in a white/blue sky And there
on the horizon is the woman who writes
Saskatchewan this strange word
at once sinuous and thorny A woman
who is one small puff of dust
at the edge of the screen
moving steadily across the sepia film
to a soundtrack heavily reliant
on guitars
                    She writes back
          You will see the wild horses

divided highway

The man who owns the paving company
loves the land. He strokes his maples,
shows you where his owls live, where
the deer come down to drink. His eyes
widen when he speaks of sunsets,
the fire of arbutus clinging
to the site of his next subdivision.
He keeps pet trout, leans against
the cookhouse cedar like an old friend,
forgetting highways. None of his acres
is paved.

road work

1.

When the long road is empty in every direction
when miles pulse through you
regular as breath
you and the mist become the passing thoughts
of a mountain

The road and the river are your blood
You drive to keep it flowing
through places built from awkward alphabets
through warm rain roping trees to sky
faster and longer into clean wet light

2.

I pulled you over ma'am
to ask you why you are not speeding

This secondary artery is well-maintained
and wide   The corners are precisely banked
Your car
looks capable of anything

Besides
the damn road is deserted

Psychology I have to say
has always intrigued me
Don't be misled by the gloss
on my uniform shoes

3.

After the first week
all you expect of the road
is an ending   the wonder
of being stationary

Then there are gifts:
   dry wood   full moon
   a motel where
   everything works

4.

Yeah I'm not crazy about offices
I'd rather hold this Stop sign till my arm
drops off than make the coffee
for some jerk who wears a tie

One guy always has to make a pass   You'd think
they'd be used to women out here by now
but most of the crew's okay

Sure it's wet or hot or freezing cold and some days
everything tastes like asphalt
but the money's good

If I hear one more joke about soft shoulders I will
just
scream

5.

Driving here is one long prayer

Car into road
road into rock
rock into cloud and then
the sky
and one lone hawk

all of us

climbing

beats jesus

The Queen on the wall
serenely caped and much
much younger
presiding over BLTs
and truckers
tourists and home-made pie

Beats curly cardboard signs that read
Guns Don't Kill People...
No Shirt, No Shoes, No Service
Beats Stars 'n Stripes
and Rebel flags
and Jesus and the spinning racks
of *Good News!* pamphlets
Beats flypaper
Beats Elvis

salient

Above the river
desiccated streets and hard-baked buildings
offered to the sun
on griddles of stone

Nothing can hide

Trees
fend for themselves
Ubiquitous petunias thrive
on dish-slops and dog piss

In the humming burning summer silence
water
whispers only in the graveyard
tantalizing hiss

The living lick their lips think
of envying the dead

campfire songs

1.

Work of the day:

the wood the water
consider the chatter
of jays
stay warm stay dry try
to stay clean
the deer prints
the black fox the water
the wood

2.

The undeniable urge to see
the world consumed
safely
ashes to ashes
if the terms
are right
and the process
visually
pleasing

3.

Earthquake

      a log
      shifting under flame

4.

Around you the still ranks
of pine
Beyond them the absence of light
that is the lake

Duller
       duller:
the embers sadden
die

You are aware of every needle
falling in the dark

madly through mountains

*I can preserve my health and spirits by strolling
through the woods and over the hills and fields
absolutely free from worldly engagements.*
                              —Henry David Thoreau, *Walden*

1.

Driving madly through mountains,
flooded creeks and lakes
and marshes—foolish June trip
after heavy winter, and hot.
Bloody hot. Scorching asphalt,
smouldering air, but pre-mosquito,
middling traffic, practically
post-snow.
Mad to drive
through water that deep, mountains this fast,
high on a blistered road, parched
and so thirsty for a well-treed end.

2.

Nothing like a semi to sing you to sleep,
vibrato Dopplered into rolling waves,
regular enough to push you off
a drowsy cliff, plunge you
beneath those mesmerizing wheels,
beneath the high-beam night.
Ride the asphalt liquified to one strong current
into the sea of evergreens, tops waving silver
in the backwash of Slumber Queens.

3.

No alarm clock like a downgrade train,
a groan shaking rock, a keening
through trees.
                    Awake
before sun and mountain goats,
avenging insects and tin-can campers
to hear the semis,
still rolling, farting through passes;
a break in the convoy,
and two blithe birds.

transitive

When a river is wide enough and empty it is impossible
to gauge its speed surface smooth as an otter's coat
the only turmoil where its edges brush the banks the way
the hem of a woman's evening gown can stir the dust in men.
Stately: ponderous and even gentle: a very slow verb: this
is the bearing of a thoroughly wide river travelling light.

And you who would not count on a woman's calm skin
a man's broad back for one split-second of security or truth
lay your body in perfect faith upon this water you've never
met before and trust it will not move you. Forgetting

that rivers run inexorably to oceans, and the verb is apt.

the aspen knows this

That the sun dies quickly
barely a pause between
green sap and bitter gold

One breathless morning the killdeer
are gone
then the ducks
The lake is sharp withdrawn

Silence
moves coldly across the sky

reunions
(for Gay)

In the kitchen she has scrubbed
(because it's been 10 years and I have probably changed),
her stories are of cattle and their power to wound.

She tells me

>   of the cow who would not be milked,
>   would not be milked in spite of everything,
>   returning pressure for pressure by
>   cracking her ribs;
>   about the auction codes
>   signalling to savvy bidders which cow
>   is trouble, which bull
>   will kill them if it can.

My wonder amuses her.
She wonders where I've been and where I am now,
how foreign the words will be with which
I explain absence.

>   One by one her calves sickened,
>   every day another case of staph. The truck
>   included her in its round of death,
>   every day the sound of the tailgate slamming
>   while she sat in this kitchen, curtains drawn,
>   stiff back to the window.

The dogs and horses, ducks, exotic geese,
distance from the city growing in her eyes—
her life has been a preparation for this chain
of other lives: bacon home-grown and cured, eggs
fresh from the barn.

She tells me

   she has seen descendants of the cow who jumped
   the moon rise like steeplechasers
   above the railings of the pens,
   heavy hurdlers on their way to freedom;
   how the calf saved by caesarean
   weighed no more to her than a particularly
   beautiful feather or fresh snow.

I tell her
I have missed her.

bulls

Move, she says. A hell of a bull
is coming in.

But there he stands, the man who can't accept safety
from a woman, as the bull swings off the truck
and down the chute,

stops to lean his military weight
against the farmer, presses and rubs him
against the bars until the metal bends
and the man with it, turns absently
to face the shouting and the open gate, leaving
a rasp of a man in shredded overalls
weeping, welded upright to the pen.

sacrament

On your knees
fingering the sunday-dimes of soil
only the elevator pillars holding up
undecorated sky

The thurifying wind the chants
of grass and ice and flax   seed
of a good harvest
in the flat of your hand

Take   eat   this is
the body of your land
stained-glass fields
and mortgaged covenants

Drink
the sacramental air and
a proper measure of fear
swallowing hard

point of reference

Someone came here sunset after sunset,
walled his firepit with stone
cached his wood under tarp and rock.
He levelled steps down to the white-
rimmed shore, cleared a bathing channel,
marked out paths.

Someone came here night after frozen night.
The stars ignored him.
His carefully constructed fire was a fleck
of mica in the sea of pewter aspen.
The shadow of the lake below this point
would not reflect his laboured definitions.

Perhaps when he could find no more to do
he sat. Just sat. Let the distance
overcome him, the hardness of the land
and sky. Perhaps after many nights
he left more lightly than he came:
assured of what he wasn't, knowing
what he didn't need to build.

sage hills

Hours since they set out through sage
and bunchgrass windflowers hidden
roses the sweet morning wind
attentive to their sweat
Over one rolling ridge
and down into the sheltered
cup before the next and up
the shallow slope clothing stitched
and itching with the sharp seeds of
late summer and at the crest
a view
of another ridge
also grassy also rolling
but higher slightly higher
with a prospect of cooler wind
and completion

They could turn again
once they were sure the horizon
had nothing left to keep from them
once they could say with certainty
We climbed we saw we know
Then what pleasure
to turn again
ankles flayed for a story
a story that would bear repeating
We walked a long time they could say
but the view was worth it

The next ridge rolls
toward them
bunchgrass clutches
their shins the robber wind
of afternoon sucks at their sweat

They may fall like stones through the
thick sage air with everything still
as hidden as the roses

wanuskewin

We pick at the graves
of the land   The bones
leave us restless with regret

How was it here
to our fathers who tipped the scales
pale profitable men who broke the circles
of sustenance   found nothing inside
                     bison
          the burnished grass
worth recognizing

How is it now

The land is still
dying to please us   patiently dressed
in barbed wire   breathing shallow
Its people died for a dollar cross
their epitaphs carefully not saying
as much as they could

always toward mountains
(for Alex)

I am looking for your landscape
through Earl Grey Southey Sareth
the roads straightforward the heights
of the horizon subtle through Dafoe
through Leroy the elevators quiet the rivers
not making a fuss and all small graves
defended by silence

The hills are rolling even-tempered
with the odd dip down to flat water

And just as I reach you
you bend the road west
your round face pulling me past Humboldt
Bruno Biggar westward through the unambiguous sky
always always
toward mountains

romancing the stone

romancing the stone
(for Enid and Ralph)

1. Rare earth

I have stolen your stories:
a web of journeys west from Ontario,
lines describing your quest for the perfect peak,
ideal water,
the baby a bright pennon on her father's back,
the miles you walked, the drivers
who responded to the family portrait you presented,
the 66 acres you fell upon like prisoners starved for light,
a good meal of beauty within your reach at last.
You could stop here,
where mountains blotted out the memory
of asphalt and exhaust. Moons and goats
on glowing limestone cliffs,
space to draw your own new lines—in ink,
in paint—and the air, green
as the fresh jade river below you,
carrying you to ever higher altitudes.
The deer came, found safety, stayed.
Snow encompassed you.
You worked,
and woke each morning satisfied.

2. Monument

The house must look after itself,
you declare. No artificial light, no running water,
no telephone, no cracks
in its solid walls of self-sufficiency:
two by fives—plank on plank—
so stout they drown out
even the river's high-water chorus.
From the front deck, ponds and martens,
bears; from the back door, deer,
woodpeckers, the silent groves of fir.

Leaving is necessary,
sometimes for a year or two. But the house
rests in your pocket like a lucky coin,
in your blood like some ancestral song.
It is always there, its aspect modest,
foundations impregnable.

3. On the Blaeberry

Time is a shallow concept here,
the round old clock a foreigner
with an irritating accent.
Time, water-strider, inching across
the still pellucid ponds of your good days.
Columbine grows faster than you move.
Wild strawberries and borage, cama
and wood violet surge past you,
sinking into earth again before
the first cup of coffee enlivens your veins,
before the muscles of your mouths
can form three similes for
beautiful.

Suddenly—the moon.

In the city, they would say you'd lost a day.
Here, no such thing
as loss. Just circles, cycles, mandalas—
uncaring of the precise hour, the number
of grains through the waisted glass.
Nothing diminished, nothing marked.
No ticking.

4. *Figurative Landscape: The Three Sisters* by Enid Petherick

Three women immured in jagged rock
strain under the slopes, power
in their necks and arms and a monumental sadness.
They have been so long invisible,
their roundnesses and strength submerged there
down long muffled years.
Now, restless and made apparent by your hand,
they lift their heads against the immemorial pressure.
The women are rising, straightening their backs,
sadness subsumed in the exultation
of breaking stone,
about to stand up to the sky.

5. Lines to the heart

You plunge onto the deluged highway,
a tense ten-hour trip,
carrying her frames and canvases,
the raw materials of love transported
to mountains where she will metamorphose
peaks to bone and muscle, paint to light,
your urban nerves to silk.
Adrenalin your fuel, you speed
along the curved black lines that tie you
to your valley, a skein of tangled furious threads
wrapped round your heart.

One quick gulp of the free air up there,
one respite from concrete. Then
ten hours back, bearing her new images
with care. Her life, your life,
embodied in these fragile pigments,
these breakable frames.
She can make visible what fails you
in words. You want to sing
as you drive. You allow yourself one backward glance,
then turn your mind sternly
to city duty. Days later,
as you sweep the glass from asphalt,
cigarette butts from floors, her mountains,
your mountains, will keep you sane.

painting the rock

Alone on the highway
his working day as good as over
he chooses one last rock for its size the energy
of its graffiti
Driving slowly along the verge flashers on
    This one just a high-school grad splash
    That one the usual *DL luvs CJ*
      inside the ubiquitous heart
      and *Jesus Saves!* is not what he's looking for

He craves
the chalks the aerosol acrylics
letters so styled they make obscenity
seem beautiful For these
he leaves the sprayer in the truck
unwraps his brushes honouring effort
by the pains he will take
to obliterate it

Latex seems too easy and oil base
takes so long to dry he is denied
a second coat He wishes
the contractor would spring for some enamel
has thought of buying it himself
for the pleasure of its melting
juicy brushstrokes satin texture
against the coarse-grained rock

Back and forth He has his stroke down
to perfection is good at pointillism
where the deep-pocked surface indicates
irregular technique Sometimes he traces
the burning letters runs different shades
of grey around their outlines
fills block interiors then gradually expands his canvas
working outward to the rock-face edge
Sometimes he tries to match the granite's grain
but his palette is so spare
    No blacks no whites

Back and forth His wrist
is aching and his shoulders hurt
Back and forth back and
forth in the red light of
the disappearing Turner sun

Later in the bar
he tells his friends he is an artist
and laughs so they know he is only joking
though with every layer of grey
his conviction grows

He would know what to do with colour

maestro

You are busy
conducting mountains

Sweat flies from your arms
pools in my cupped hands

You turn your attention
to the clouds encouraging
the thunder with
small gestures

I feed your sweat
to the sickly flower in my garden

While you are tuning redwoods
my flower dies

Once again I have been taken in
by appearances

facets

Sunlight through window shatters
your diamond into a galaxy of colour.
On impulse, in a breath of laughter and euphoria,
you press its facets against the pane, scribe
your initials in one corner, asserting
that this moment will last forever, for nothing
is more steadfast than diamond.

The sun strikes sparks from the incised glass,
the still diamond—which, within its adamantine heart-of-hearts,
struggles for equilibrium in this shallow world.
You, your lover, the glass itself
will, relatively soon, sink into stone, carbon and silica,
a nourishing sand. And diamond, shape-shifter
after thirty thousand surficial years, will make its mark
on the long thesis of impermanence,
telling the story of universal change
in the soft black voice of graphite.

granite

I have prepared so thoroughly
for your death that your voice
sharp as always on the phone
pierces upward from a depth
like memory disconcerts me

Stubborn
you refuse to die to doctors' orders
and you will win in the end

leave me with bone-deep knowledge
of granite
and other hard places

plutons

Daily they rise in us,
magmas of desire and expectation
unfulfilled, hot rocks of frustration stopped
short on the dark side of crusts accreted
over lives that feel as long as geological time.
There they solidify, undigested cores
of what could be knowledge, given a little air.
What could be murder,
given a tectonic tremor or a little more steam.
Read the papers: the day trader,
the over-heated teens. The incendiary urge
to burn our names on the sky.

word from the roots

1.

The word from the roots is
live
thrust brush
aside break
down all
impediments

Form is brittle
All attitudes assumed
since germination are brittle
Shattering
is possible

2.

The word you hear from the roots
is your mother's voice
speaking through strong white tendrils
in the cause of order:
clean your plate

Nothing to do
with nourishment

The word is:
recognize the rules
the right to make rules
rulers

3.

Roots shatter asphalt
buckle sidewalks
peristalsis of destruction
in the cause of
progress:
new leaves/new territory:
advance
gain ground
prevail

4.

The word from the roots
is *open open open*
Air flows
light waves
sun enwraps and coaxes

Your unnatural blindness:
pores closed
fault
of a city heart

5.

Pollinate germinate and
reproduce and you
do none of these

Congress
does not become you
stopping your ears

to save your mind
Oneness
in a singular sense

6.

Under your self-conscious
shoes under these delicate and
well-recorded willows
roots are shouting
feed
me

7.

You scrape the topsoil
now and then
become entangled
in intemperate subsurface
threads:

sharp hearts and daggers of
clichéd tattoos:
Mother
initials and aggressive snakes:
painful
expensive to remove

aftershock

The shock
when rock we build on rebounds unfolds
to make us face the nerves and blood
of what we thought insentient

Then we remember darkness
the inconstancy of fire run
from the dread of
old unholy voices:
   ambulances
   howling at the moon

this way to the hermit

The sign said *This way to the hermit*
so we went
It was a slow day in August
nothing to get excited about
just lightning and some US tourists
It was a long path steep in places
but most of us kept up
Where's the snack bar? said the tourists
and *What? No drinking fountains?*

Part of the trail collapsed
Two women in tweed shorts
dropped off and then there was
some business about a snake
One bald old man I never saw again
A bear appeared and several people
fainted We left them
It was getting late We didn't want
to miss the Texas barbecue

But just when we began to feel
a little lonely (the sun was low now
everywhere just rocks
turning a godawful red
and we were thinking of some strong words
for the Parks Department) we saw
a thin man
sitting
in the middle of the cliff

Hey we shouted
are you the hermit?

He sat up straight and
stared at us   *Hey* we said
say something good and then
we've got to go back down
Our bus is waiting

He laughed and laughed
He shook all over
I never saw a human laugh so hard
He fell right off the cliff and we
could hear him laughing down
a thousand feet or so

Then Mike said   *Well enough of this*
I'm heading back   and Rob
and June said *Right*
and Sandy looked at me and said
C'mon then and they started off

And me
I couldn't seem to move a foot
What did he eat up there?
What happened when it snowed and what
was he laughing at?

It's been a week or two
maybe a month who counts
up here   The stars
are pretty scary but the moon
grows on you

traverse

She traverses shattered limestone. Insanity is this solitary clutching at a shivered outcrop decomposing in the sweat of her hands. Pure reason is each considered step, mind probing the chips and cobbles to the parent rock, ganglia meeting the threads of life there, twining round them till she is no longer solitary. This is love and fear and growing up. Fear of the sparks her hammer strikes flying to meet the dry moss dry grass dry cones and twigs to either side. Fear of conflagration, love of terror. Her dry lips, her desert skin. The world will burn like noon sun through pure marble and she the (tenuous) cause. Shakti, high on a mountain, and so small. A pebble she dislodges will plunge like a disappointed heart, striking cobbles which will roll inexorably at boulders, a hard and heavy rain of stone upon the road below, filling the valley, sinking the river and its lakes, rolling, rolling, till the rock face is bare and she can see her bones, her mother's bones, all her skeletons in the stripped stern mountain, the adamant wall she clings to as the fanciful green world disappears.

forest of daughters

class of '62

The woman who ran the 100-yard dash
faster than you had ever seen a woman run
is fat
and hurt that you don't recognize her

The farm kids still have red cheeks at 40
and you're hurt because they do recognize you
You have changed beyond all recognition
have been places can't possibly resemble
the high-school photo pinned
to your lapel

Teachers size you up
collect on bets with themselves
They talk to you as if you are
the adult you thought you were when you walked in

Your smile aches You circle conversations
and wonder where you really were
the night the bus died and you all waded home
clutching your floor-length formals
above the snow or the time your best friend
got so drunk you left her in a tidy parcel
on her mother's doorstep rang the bell
and ran

This
is not your movie

The music is sweet and silly
You have forgotten how to jive
The boy who fought you for first place in English
is a bitter socialist who objects to your jewellery
The guy you secretly adored is bald
and will never play basketball again

Behind the layers and lines a few ghosts linger
Their presence is too poignant
to be borne sober   Young eyes shine past you
at a future that is nothing like this

Nothing like

curriculum mortis

My years are as smooth as
new mirrors, *she said.*
There are no notable events
to speak of. Few days
stand out.

I go to work, and then
go home.
I garden.
I saw a film
when the Tube strike stranded me
in town.

I have one parent,
one cat,
one friend.
I dress in a well-cut
conservative manner.
I would rather not be noticed.

The hours pass quickly,
very smoothly.
I am, of course,
content. I am amazed sometimes
how quickly hours pass.
Yes, very quickly.
Ever so smoothly.

Really.

lessons

I thought of you at once when I saw them dancing:
gazes locked, smiles pasted,
flashing in over-practised swoops.
But beautiful,
       beautiful anyway.

I thought of your thin shoes, unstylish jacket.
Your knees, you told me, ached so much at night,
it was a trial to sleep. Your students
noticed nothing. They had the dream, the movie—
themselves in feathered gowns, you in a tux,
       champagne and applause

And you, imagining them weightless and adept,
overcame their lonely gravity and gave them
sixty minutesful of grace. They flirted gratefully,
they got their money's worth,
       and told their friends.

Now watching these smooth polished feet, two bodies
in single breath-like motion, I recall
midnight excursions to hidden clubs:
red tablecloths and miniscule parquet floors
and the joy you took in dancing then,
with me, because you didn't
       have to dance.

strut

Those were the legs! kicking at the sun
in skirts as brief as conversations with
your parents in shorts no longer than a haiku
breath Hi-steppin over father's frowns and
mother's blushes those legs were never
going to stop for anything Legs up to the
armpits Legs like Lucille Ball had and
still has for all you know kicking clouds
out of her way Legs like endless summer
endless drive-in movies like everything
you think will never end when you're
17 and stepping out

kate and friends: 14

Forest of daughters,
all copper-toned limbs
and honeyed hair,
bees in their blood, nights filled
with excited wings.

Wands of tall daughters,
shining, slender,
tender to any wind
that bears a hint of doubt;
rough
against fences.

Navels pierced,
and their hearts, daily.

Stretched and golden:
see how they cluster,
sway apart, bend and spring
for the sun.

juvendous

You might break this new world
in your haste to love it
Your teeth tremble with each taste
It's a grape that will burst
with a little more
pressure

How long can you keep
a life this ripe intact
between your unlined palms

Why not
shatter it now
your nerves are saying
then there'll be nothing
left to fear

The tension
    in your jaw
    cramped hands
is terrible

One
small movement
A muscle spasm

The pieces
will be yours to play with

elemental
(for Alanna)

You came in like a lion that March morning,
tearing your mother's flesh, a Serengeti of a wind
already roaring through you. It amplified
your keen-edged voice till no restaurant would let us
stay, it stiffened you against our hugs and strokes
and left you parched with want
for something, something...

That wind hasn't died. It only falls from time to time,
deceptive lulls. Taller than your mother now,
you never seem to know which way its gusts
will take you. We watch you veer
from equatorial sun to nordic dark, glad
of your strong body, wishing you an equal strength
of mind, daylight friendships, pleasures not stolen.

Wind at your back, you leap away from us
toward some Disney sunrise of sixteen, visions of car keys
jingling in your hand and a destination that is anywhere
but here, a place whose walls are black one day,
white the next, may or may not have windows—
yours to change, now. All we can do
is wait behind the dunes our own winds carved,
shivering.

day surgery

  Soft needles
and behind your eyelids the rioting shoes
size 13A thick soles and bulbous toes
These are your cells they single out and
pop like grapes like fallen
stars

All the circuits etched in silver and bruises
are busy now   Please
              Are you feeling pain?
disconnect and dial again

  Stomach lifts
like a heart enduring rainbows
and here is one
  all the grave shades
  of death and muchmusic
  misted with human voices
          speaking coolly of gardens
          and your frozen skin
while fast-frame roses open
like hungry mouths
spitting petals at your eyes your eyes

and your feet float above your
melted bones swaying to the voices
that sing to you
          It's over
               over
          The cuts
          have been accomplished
          Rest here
               not too long
          throw up and
          go home

jerry-built

How frail and thinly skinned we are
and lacking

Running upright insecure and gangly
dangling everywhere What can we ever
catch with our elbows flapping bobbing heads
What can we scramble up undamaged
that any solid animal
back reverently level to the soil
can't scale in one seamless breath

Our flawed unfluid skeletons

These awkward organs

Even our famous brain aches at times
corroding what it touches

Fingers may work for a while
like promises kept   bind
build fire grasp at the moon and knives

Till the morning when cold water burns
the small bones swell
against the blood and skin

That cold morning
when nothing can be held or tied
and rust by design sets in
to more than our fragile spines

mileage

Her dog has died
a friend is dying
Her bones ache and no one will listen to her
as if she was loved

These grey days

Who would have thought them possible?
Not her at sixteen   not her
at thirty-five or even fifty

The garden is overgrown

Her hair is thinning

Time is speeding
toward a canyon she has dreamt of
Time is dragging
like an injured wing

If only events had reversed themselves
the worst first
easier to take when she was younger stronger
and not so tired
She wants to roll years backward
like mileage on a crooked dealer's car lot
She is fairly sure she didn't choose
to grow old this way

It rains and rains

The garden grows

She cries
at the news of another spring

dahlias

She marks the plants she will give space to
next year, those she will throw to the forest
to grow wild. The erect yellows stay;
these tight purples are no trouble at all.
But the flaming orange droop and sprawl,
cannot adapt themselves to this small garden.
It's not their fault they reach so high,
that their pace outruns their strength.
She'll miss their colour, exclamation marks
of fire, the exclamations of her visitors.
But she is too old now for staking, tying,
bracing up. This is life, she says:
doing what is possible, abandoning
the uncontrollable.
The day is hot. She is tiring fast,
but cold is coming and she needs to know
her garden is in order.

cut and set

She chats to the woman
in the next chair and does not recognize
herself in the wide mirror
sitting straight bright-eyed and happy
She even likes the neon music
the bitter coffee in its fluorescent purple mug

She'd come here twice a month
if pensions went a little farther
But saving strictly can at least
buy her this loud necessary warmth
every six weeks or so

Her hairdresser has such a pretty face
under that wild red mop
and touches her so gently
fingers talented at massage
at patting a caped shoulder

She imagines her grand-daughter's hands
might reassure like this
if she had a grand-daughter:
fingertips stroking the nape of her neck
to get the cut line right the soft brush
purring along her scalp lifting her hair
to the fuller days when it didn't cost her
$40 to be touched

bodies of evidence

1. Palimpsest

This waking to your mother's mirror
this double-take
the family template a sudden second skin

You'd like to blame the light which is unusually
stark this morning and the mirror
which is exceptionally clean
You want to swear this surface is a mask you can sweat off
with a few more pushups and a firmer will

But memory flips through photo albums
stopping at a neck you recognize a set of knuckles
swollen with what you know is portent
Etchings
recorded there a hundred years ago

The images are faded though
faint enough for hope

2. Libration

These three were daddies' girls
running past their mothers toward the smell of pipe tobacco
and the tall men who could lift them with one arm
who read thick books said *yes* to dogs when mothers had said *no*
taught them to swim and spoke of college and other countries

Mothers were blurs in unsurprising kitchens
so faded that daughters had to reinvent them
using soft dull scraps of boredom particles of rage

One by one
fathers have died
leaving daughters inconsolable in boardrooms
From these they venture back travel for miles
to climb front steps of formerly male addresses
to meet in daylight porch-light hall-light the shadowed women
who were always waiting for them

3. Heirloom

Her mother died two years ago
uncomplaining
of the knives in her hips
the hot lead in her stomach

Sorting through her mother's clothes
the daughter plays dress-up with funereal scarves
pulls this history of pain on over her head
as smoothly as a well-worn jersey dress
Makes its colours strident

4. Patinas

My father hates to be told he is looking well
and counters with his feet his back his heart

But he does look well
younger and more rested than my mother
in spite of paraplegia coma epilepsy
50 years of raging at the accidents of war

This should be fair
   the smooth surface of the well-looked-after
   some small reward for injury
   and an interrupted mind

This should be fair
but isn't
   A man's skin silkened to serenity
   A woman's ragged with the worry of him

gemini

When you speak,
I hear my father's voice.
In young photos, you are the shorter by two inches,
the one without the grin.

Family legend has it that I cried
each time you left, stretched my boneless hand
toward your moustache, your military beret.

I have always left you sadly, guessing
that a broken father would be easier to bear
without you there, a whole and upright
mirror image.

Now you too are breaking. You sway; your heart
fails you. Your breath is fragile,
sleep is terrifying.

You with your cane, my father with his crutch,
stand together under what could be
your penultimate spring sun.
You, still slimmer; he, still taller.
Your heads are fine and silver.
Parting, your matching hands grip hard,
your right, his left, through the window of the car:
veins prominent, nails enviably oval.

I will remember you both like this—
bodies alike again after fifty distinct years,
the love in your eyes.

rounds

Make sure the drawbridge
is drawn up the shutters firmly latched
dogs unleashed
the fires damped

Preserve us as we sleep my gods
Protect this house and all within
Protect those under
my protection

And so my father
shuffling in pain to his apartment door
tries the knob with his one good hand
peers
to make sure of the chain

my mother's birds

Her hands are small birds,
terrified and pulsing.

Shoulders square
in dignified repose,
dependable and calm, all of her—
except these threatened sparrows
at the end of her wrists,
almost dancing
to a tune she will not hear of,
staccato, and grave.

cedar

This cedar is my father now,
straighter and stronger than he has been
in years. More flexible
and yielding.
The grit of his old bones
scratched my fingers as I sowed it here.
Wind took the finer dust and spread it
farther than I could, well beyond my reach,
as he always was.
But I have him now, rooted in my territory:
a trunk I can embrace
without pain. His rough skin
cannot shrink from me, his limbs are gifts.

lightly

My mother walked the Nottinghamshire fields
as if she was dancing, stepping lightly
over cowslips, leaping ditches, pliéing
to pick some mauve flower pinned
like a discarded scrap of tulle
to the coarse grass.

This in a childhood, thick with duty,
she thinks not worth dwelling on.

My mother walked on the tips of her toes
through stately polished homes in her plain
white apron, spinning to avoid the butler,
unenvious of the lives that waltzed upstairs
and into the Sunday papers.

This is her portrait
on the occasion of the Royal Albert Servants' Ball:
hair finger-waved and eyes convinced
there would always be music somewhere.

My mother still steps lightly
with feet as gnarled and wrenched as those
of any ballerina, her backbone crumbling
but strong enough to keep her world upright.
Agnes DeMille, she tells me, danced
till her shoes were filled with blood.

I don't know how they do it, she says,
never looking back at her footprints.

acknowledgements

Thanks to the periodicals, anthologies and other media that first accepted many of these pieces, sometimes in slightly different forms:

Anthology of New England Writers, 1995
The Antigonish Review
Cicada
Contemporary Verse 2
Event
The Fiddlehead
Grain
The Malahat Review
The New Quarterly
Prairie Journal of Canadian Literature
Prism international
Quintet: Themes & Variations, Ekstasis Editions
Room of One's Own
sub-TERRAIN
Vintage '92 Anthology, League of Canadian Poets
Wascana Review
Zygote

Great gratitude to Evelyn Lau for her years of truth, friendship and sacred journeys.

And special thanks to the other members of Quintet—Pam Galloway, Eileen Kernaghan, Jean Mallinson and Clélie Rich—for their sharp pencils and wide horizons.

SUE NEVILL is the author of *I Was Expecting Someone Taller*, and a co-author of *Quintet: Themes & Variations*. Her poetry has been widely published in such Canadian literary periodicals as *The Antigonish Review*, *CV2*, *Event*, *The Fiddlehead*, *Grain*, *The Malahat Review* and *The New Quarterly*. Nevill's work has appeared in many anthologies, including *The Windhorse Reader: Choice Poems of 1993*. She is a longtime resident of Vancouver, BC.